POETRY now

Upon Life's Pedestal

Edited by

Heather Killingray

First published in Great Britain in 2005 by
POETRY NOW
Remus House,
Coltsfoot Drive,
Peterborough, PE2 9JX
Telephone (01733) 898101
Fax (01733) 313524

SB ISBN 1 84460 868 9

FOREWORD

Although we are a nation of poets we are accused of not reading poetry, or buying poetry books. After many years of listening to the incessant gripes of poetry publishers, I can only assume that the books they publish, in general, are books that most people do not want to read.

Poetry should not be obscure, introverted, and as cryptic as a crossword puzzle: it is the poet's duty to reach out and embrace the world.

The world owes the poet nothing and we should not be expected to dig and delve into a rambling discourse searching for some inner meaning.

The reason we write poetry (and almost all of us do) is because we want to communicate: an ideal; an idea; or a specific feeling. Poetry is as essential in communication, as a letter; a radio; a telephone, and the main criterion for selecting the poems in this anthology is very simple: they communicate.

Contents

Determined By The Term

Your fate is determined by the term,
Will you suffer the determination
For a termination
Or make it full-term?
Are you just a foetus or a child
Worth the ongoing fight?
Or just a parasite
Not worth sentiment mild?
Change the word, the term you use,
From non-human foetus
To human, one of us,
And suddenly it's not a procedure
Like a medical cure
But lethal child abuse.
A word makes a world of difference:
Such as subhuman Jews
Were animals to death-camp screws
Worthy of indifference.
Call it a baby
Then just maybe
It is murder and not
Abortion that you have got
On your conscience
And a simple word is no defence?
Or does the change
Modify the range
So sentiment is folly
And you justify yourself
For the good of your health
As you lay upon the trolley?

D J Tyrer

World Of Injustice

Another year will soon have passed
Into historic oblivion
The situation in Iraq and Israel
Just goes on and on
The people in these countries
Are innocent, like you and me
But as in times of bygone days
'Tis plain for all to see
They are the ones who suffer most
From tyrannical beasts
And while the remains of their regime
Are still alive and well
Left to their own devices
They'll blow every westerner to Hell
But if evil is to be overcome
The good Lord should cause their demises
But the ways of the world go on and on
We have no say in that
So hands together, say our prayers
And hope our island doesn't fall flat!

Georgie Woodshaw

Winter

Outside the snow has fallen thick
The countryside is covered
As though a blanket's fallen down
And everything is smothered

The trees, their branches covered white
Like stardust, they are gleaming
The mountaintops are shining bright
And all around is freezing.

The birds, they flutter to and fro
In search of food among the snow
But there is none that can be found
The snow has covered all the ground.

But as the winter passes by
The trees stand out against the sky
They make a scene one can't forget
Of 'nature' with its own 'sunset'

Dennis Corkin

NIGHT

Softly she sheds her coloured hues,
Appears the dark mysterious blue of night,
Gently enfolding all around.
Gone is the harshness of light.
Silvery glint of her friend the moon,
Lends opal sheen
Upon the winding river,
Where from wily fish we glean.
Sounds are muted, and as the world in slumber lay,
The owl emerges to start his day.

Edna Freeland

Six Feet Deep

It seems so long I fell asleep
And woke up here: six feet deep.
How could they think that I was dead
When merely resting on my bed?
How could the soil and wood encase
This lifeless, undead, resting place?
Raging, at first, I beat the wood
And screamed the loudest that I could;
But all my thuds, and all my calls
Were smothered inside the coffin walls.
And so, lying here, with every breath
Drawing me closer to my death,
I try to think of cool sea air -
The way its touch ran through my hair;
Or the sight of fields in summer sun -
Their fragrant fumes when day is done.
But here those joys cannot stay -
Like old cobwebs, they waste away.
Darkness is my sole reality:
It is all I feel - all I see.
Indeed, I wonder, has life been
More than a dark, lonely coffin?
As my body withers to bone,
I pray this is written on my stone:
Here is nothing - do not weep,
We all live lives six feet deep.

Matthew Graham Scarsbrook

I Wish I Now Were Thin

I used to be so slim and lithe,
Would dance the cha-cha, and love to jive,
My full skirts swung as round I'd spin,
Oh, how I wish I now were thin.

I so enjoyed to run and swim,
At the water's edge, the pebbles skim.
Not a sign of a double chin,
Oh, how I wish I now were thin.

I used to eat ice cream and jam,
Roast spuds, mint sauce with juicy lamb,
I always ate the fatty skin,
Oh, how I wish I now were thin.

My children kept me on the go,
When small, they'd never heard of 'slow'.
At night relaxed with a double gin,
Oh, how I wish I now were thin.

The boys, now fathers, racing round,
Keeping fit on the football ground,
Their wives fit from the workout gym,
Oh, how I wish I now were thin.

Arthritis stops the knees from kneeling,
The back won't bend, each joint has feeling,
What else in store can old age bring?
Oh, how I wish I now were thin.

It's not the style of what's the rage,
It's just the weight to match the age,
For come the time they lift me in,
Then all will wish I now were thin.

Monica D Buxton

DREAMS ARE FUN

It is fun to dream
And live in another world
Without the constraints
Of this mortal Earth
The freedom that exists
Behind closed eyes
Is just enough
To please a tired mind
The result being
Joy and happiness
So it is fun to dream
In fact it's the best.

Matthew Holloway

A Fox's Point Of View

Please don't chase me,
Please don't take away my sun;
I know this is what you do just for fun
But my life has just begun.
If you could just leave it for another day,
I could be on my way.
Your weapons are too much for me to take,
I wouldn't hurt you so why do you stay?

I kill my prey but I have to;
I have to survive like my mummy says,
I don't want to, it's not fun,
I would never deprive anything of seeing its next sun.

If I could talk I would tell you
To leave me alone and go away,
But all I have is my beauty
So in the end come what may.

I was going to watch a sunset tonight;
My first one ever, sit and watch it or lay,
But now I might never get the chance,
If your weapons you don't delay.

Maybe one day someone will help me,
Make people listen and this will stop.
I know there are people that try to help me,
So if someone is trying to, please listen . . .
Listen to what they say,
You can't hear my thoughts,
But their thoughts turned to words, you may.

The more people that listen,
The more chance I have of getting away.
If they really try hard to help,
I could see my first sunset one day . . .
Please don't chase me

Only you can make them go away . . .

Georgina May Carey

High Time

The journey of the ticking clock
Takes all day long.
Seconds flutter past
And hours mutter on.
Its journey never seems finished
And its chiming carries on,
As I stand and face
The face of it
With its long and sombre song.
It has no beginning
Or daring end in sight,
But it ticks and tocks
And clicks its cogs
'Till it chimes', its quarters mock.
Now I don't bother
To worry 'bout the time,
In any kind of weather
It'll tick away just fine.

Ruth Le Goff

You Are My Rock

In troubled times, you are always there
Ready with advice, and a helping hand
I look upon you, as someone, very rare
Because I know, you always, understand.

You are my rock, to whom I cling
When I struggle, and support I need
Great comfort, you will often bring
Your very existence, enables me to breathe.

When the stormy clouds gather, up above
When tempestuous waves rise, above my head
Always close at hand with warmth and love
From you, words of wisdom are often shed.

When tears are cascading, down my face
You seek to gather me, to your breast
You always stand solid, firm, in your place
Your advice and support, put my troubles to rest.

Like a mountain, you stand firm and tall
Rushing to my aid when you hear my cry
Always ready to answer a desperate call
Calming troubled waters when waves ride high.

When inner turmoil seems to be destroying my mind
When my tolerance just flies out of hand
You show great compassion, because you are so kind
Like my David, against Goliath, you will stand.

You are my fortress when gales start to blow
You are my shelter from a torrential storm
When my furrowed brow needs to vanish, I know
You banish the spirits, and help keep me warm.

While seeking no recompense, while being my guide
Our friendship will never die, because I have you at my side.

B W Ballard

A Woman's Place

Bright-eyed girl child, quick and precocious
Learn the rules, hold your tongue
Good little girls are seen and not heard
Sit quite still now, don't say a word
Put that book away, that's of little use to you
What's the point of education for a girl?
Only boys are valued in a man's world
Concentrate on learning how to cook and sew
One day you'll have a husband, you'll have children
Cleaning, keeping house - all you'll need to know
Derided, humiliated, put down, pushed around
Be respectful, know your place
No one asks for your opinions
Adults know best what's best for you
You're only a child - what do you know?

Teetering on high heels, smearing on lipstick
Painting, powdering, must attract a mate
Frantically searching, all your friends are married
You're past twenty - it's almost too late!
Must get a husband, must have children
What else are you good for?
What else can you do?
If you were left on the shelf
How could you manage by yourself?
Confidence at low ebb, self-esteem wounded
Downtrodden, browbeaten
Self-effacing, knowing your place
No one asks for your opinions
Men know best what's best for you
You're only a woman - what do you know?

Leyna Brinkmeyer

Mum Excels

Age 'twould gladden mine heart
'Twould mine mum warmeth too
An' she'd stroken locks of hair
Noted nothin' hadden changeth
But thine eyes still me knoweth
Had thee checken I'd be gladdeth.
Timeth 'twere laiden down
Rest your heart of purest gold.
To be and scattered thy family
But nay ye are walkin' too much
An' in ye prayers be answer to thine years
Yearn on ye olde and youngen
For this thy mysterious natures
Then ye olde answer'n
To the dishearten'.

Hardeep Singh-Leader

The Miracle

I saw this lovely flower,
Sprouting from the ground.
It really was a miracle,
For guess where it was found?
Not in a beautiful garden,
Or a colourful flower bed,
But amongst a rubbish tip
Was a lovely shade of red.

Everything near was colourless,
Dirty and smelly too.
But then I saw the flower,
What a fantastic hue!
I wondered how it got there.
Was it from a seed?
Maybe a bird dropped it,
Whilst it was having a feed.

No matter how it got there,
Amongst the rubbish tip,
It made a colourful display,
Where the flower now sits.
So if you think your life is dull,
Just take a look around.
See if you can find a flower
Sprouting from the ground.

Just think about that flower
He is now alone,
Among the dirt and rubble,
It's not really his home.
So, if you have a problem,
And you don't know what to do,
Find a lonely flower,
And thank God that is not you.

Doreen E Hampshire

When Two Become One

Come to Me, Robert, My love
Please use Mine eyes and ears
Reach down deep within Your heart
And spread love where once were tears

Our spirits will become entwined
When two at last become one
Our Father's hand will then bless us both
All heartache then will be gone

The world will be as spirits joined
His children full of glee
At last the world will re-unite
With Father's love, so free.

April Dickinson-Owen (A O)

WALKING

The night air was so cold as I walked home tonight
My mind filled with milky images and words
I thought an alphabet had arrived, a galaxy
New and shiny letters that I couldn't understand
They formed words like none I've ever read, words that spelled out new
Words even as I thought them into being, I had to write, I had to burn
The candle of poetry. You know what I mean and that's why I love you.

Andy Hinkinson

WALL OF SILENCE

To catch a heaven-sent teardrop in your hand
To think of its life before falling thru fingers that have experienced
an age
Caught in a beautiful cobwebbed veil
The tear silently caresses silken death in a silent voice
Finally penetrating the circle of a dwelling
A deep inhabitation, noiselessly black
To breathe reluctantly shallow depths of another's voice in a moment
As though a one-day butterfly trembles hearing the accents of flight
In the wall of silence the ugly interior swallows any observations of
remembered reality
To survive the wall, loneliness must be diminished
To reluctantly awaken after transforming breath into fragments of scent
To limit sadness thru trust
The cruel pain of the skin of silence vibrates on the web,
filling speech with peace
The colourful words finally run away from silence
As the one-day butterfly you have become escapes the wall.

Hilary Jean Clark

Anger

Have I not done my very best to help my fellow man?
Did I not follow every rule according to the plan?

Was I not first to keep the peace within the civil laws
And help the only instigator fighting for the cause?

Did I not bare my heart and soul for everyone to see?
Have I not brought the burden of compassion home with me?

Did I not open every door for those who came to call
Or scrub the broken promise from the shadows on the wall?

Did I not light the candle when the world was dark with sin?
Did I not find the courage and confront the fears within?

Did I not smooth the surface when the road became too steep
And douse the flaming embers with the teardrops that I weep?

Did I not turn the hands of time and calm the raging storm?
Did I not mop the sweating brow whenever it was warm?

Have I not roamed the universe invading every dream
And pacified the torment by relieving every scream?

What more have I to offer for this captivated mind
When underneath the surface there is nothing I can find

To hide the deprivation that is flowing with the tide
And cover up the stench that rots inside?

Ken Mulligan

Reflections

When I look into a mirror
Who do I see?
A bright bubbly chappy
Who used to be me!
Or a sad moody stranger
That has now become me?

Tablets and treatment
Have taken their toll
As I strive to make
My mind and body whole

Is there light at the end
Of the tunnel?
We shall see
Because whatever they say
What will be, will be.

The light in the tunnel
Now grows brighter
I won't give in,
'I'm a fighter'!
Will I win? We shall see!
Now when I look in the mirror
I want to see
That bright cheerful
Chappy
Smiling back at me.

Roy Perkins

For My Part

I love the way you don't put your arms around me.
I love the way you don't text me back.
I love the way you ignore
a phone message I've left.
I love the way you no longer initiate
a hug, a kiss or even sex.
I love the way we no longer do things together
and you don't seem to care
if I'm there with you or if I'm not.

I love the way we go out separately.
I love the way you no longer say you love me.
You did once. You've forgotten.
You used to say it all the time,
but memories are short.
If you said it now
you'd no longer mean it anyway.
Empty words are pointless.
For my part I wish I could just turn back the clock
to what we once had
and put whatever went wrong right.

Andy Botterill

OLDER

You and me, when we're seventy-three,
And both our partners have gone,
We will live in the same town, and have each other round
At least two times a day.
Your children's children will call me 'Nan',
I won't mind, they will and they can,
We'll remember the things we didn't do,
Forever together, me and you,
Just how it's always been.

You and I, when we're eighty-five,
We will live in the same old house,
Too old to drive, and the kids realise
That I'm not related at all.
We're just close friends, and in the end,
It's all we'll ever be.
Memories slowly turn to regret,
We may be old, but we don't forget
What we could have been.

You and me, when we're ninety-three,
Sleep in the same bed,
Finally together, lying forever,
Just where we should be.
What you promised me, when we were twenty-three,
Our last wishes never came true,
From friend to lover,
But too late to discover,
What we could have been.

Danielle Coxon

FELINE FINE

Quietly contented
Pussycat of mine
Sitting alone
All refine
Licking your nails
Thinking of mice
Destroyer of life
Not very nice
Happy old cat
Set in her ways
Sleeping all night
Wandering all day.

J M Stoles

Fool's Circle

There have been times in my life
When I doubted or lost my faith
With the death of my wife
I lost all belief in life, in God, in me.

Yet every time I get lost
Every time I cry
A voice inside says, 'Why?'
I travel in circles
Back to my roots and faith.

I lost it first after my Bar Mitzvah
I couldn't see the point
With mates of all beliefs
What was mankind fighting for?

I found it in Germany
In a synagogue surrounded by a convent
I lost it when my parents died
And found it in an extermination camp
And in the eyes of Bosnian children
I lost it when my wife was taken from this mortal plane
My friends found it and returned it to me.
I will never lose it again.

Believe what you choose to believe, but believe in it totally
Never lose your faith, whatever that may be
Don't keep travelling at angles and tangents
Do not! Travel on the 'Fool's Circle' like me

Derek Blackburn

RICHARD

Tired, but smiling
He appeared at my front door
Neither of us knew what was to come,
What fate did have in store.

Pleasant, polite, a cheeky grin
He talked non-stop at times.
He loved my dog, many hugs she got
He loved his pennies, pounds and dimes!

As time passed by,
He showed a flair at school
Praise, smiles, around him flowed
But he loved to play the fool!

Gradually, as years went by
Unreliable he became
Lies, stealing, possibly even worse
Life was never again to be the same.

At eighteen, I suggested he left
Perhaps to be happier on his own
But nothing suited this young man
And life was one long moan!

He refuses to cope and face the future
What hope is there for him?
He's exhausted relatives, friends - only one,
What can I do to help this lad?

The chances are really slim.

Elizabeth M Thom

Footsteps In Love

Love holds many unsuspecting joys.
Sweetly it comes along.
When you think all hope has gone.

I vividly retain the memory
When she took me by the hand,
And with smiling bright eyes
Kissed me passionately
And my heart beat a faster sound.

Then, we sat by a big oak tree for a while,
And embraced with ardent love and glee.

Casually we walked along the silver riverbank
And we quietly ate and drank.
Later on, she took her leave briskly -
And saying with audacity,
'I love you - so coax me in love again!'

A few weeks on:
Finally the true knot was tied
And our hearts in love shone,
For all to see as we happily
Walked by the River Wye.

Sammy Michael Davis

Life's Needs

Oh what busy lives we lead,
Yet we manage to succeed in doing all our daily tasks
And a little more when someone asks,
'Can you help me out today?'
We breathe a sigh, and say, 'OK.'

Then on those days when life seems hectic
And our minds are in a whirl,
We have no time for self so accept it.
At the end of the day we collapse in a heap,
Put on the 'tele' and fall asleep.

If we had nothing to do we'd be bored to distraction,
Life would be meaningless, empty and lonely,
So reach out and touch someone!
You'll feel satisfaction.

Give of your time, it's not just for you
For a heart of compassion is kindly and true!
So help others today and forget about you!

Gwyneth Llewellyn Rea

Down By The Sea

On Norfolk's eastern shore,
We left the train and tracked down to the sea.
Wandering along the seashelled shore,
Saltwater trickling through crimson toes.

Sand in our sandwiches, even in our tea.
Ice cream drips down our chubby chins.
Mum relaxes on her multicoloured towel,
Dad reads his book for his sins.

The golden sphere of life begins to sink on an azure sea.
While humid air wafts through our silken curls,
Temperate sand sifts through tired toes,
As we troop along the shore.

Dad cries, 'What a day it's been, but now it's time to go.'
'Oh no, just a few minutes more,' we sing.
Later on the green, ingesting freshly fried fish and chips,
Mum says, 'We'll remember today and the sweet tang of the
Incoming sea.'

We slept that night tucked up in bed,
Happy memories of surf, sea and sand still
Drifting through our heads.
Oh what a wonderful day we had had.

P R Baker

Living The Moment

Suddenly I awake hearing
the laboured breathing of
the bay mare miles away.
The miracle has begun.

Beaming headlights stroke
deserted lanes showing
the way to the stable.
A nativity beckons.

The mare gives a soft greeting,
eyes dark with kindness.
In answer to my wordless question
she steps aside to reveal

her foal, curved in foetal position
in the straw, still steaming
from blood and birth water.
I hear a bubble of breath.

A gangling of infant limbs
tapering to translucent
strands of gristle, tremble.
The foal raises its head.

I remove the placenta
stretching the tricorn out
on rimed meadow.
All complete.

Light slashes the horizon.
The cold dawn bustles with birds
living the moment.

Maggie Andrews

CARPENTER'S WIFE

Bethlehem's back streets, a young mother reaches her time,
star and shepherds and a new King born in poverty and grime.
The world will never be the same, the Word has come to life,
the promised Messiah is born, to a frightened carpenter's wife.

Bethlehem ghetto and the stable of an overcrowded inn,
the reek of cattle, festering like the stench in man's sin.
God as man made flesh, born amongst the filth and blight,
the promised Saviour is born, to a homeless carpenter's wife.

Bethlehem manger, there couldn't be a more humble start,
it speaks of identification, it speaks of the Father's heart.
God's salvation is at hand, exposing man's greed and strife,
the Lord has come, miraculously born to a carpenter's wife.

Keith Leese

A Bit Of Peace

I need a bit of quiet,
I need a bit of peace,
The pace is far too hectic,
Please give me some release.
Just give me time to ponder,
And time to give some thought,
To things that really matter,
For things that can't be bought.
I seem to be in turmoil,
From morning until night,
There's got to be a change somehow,
If not, I'll just take flight.

Enid Edmunds

PERPETUAL MOTION

Time is on my hands, I make it my own
It knows me well
A pass of time is an elapse to freedom in this world of mine
The world is what you make it
So who am I to judge the fools who don't move on?
The monotony of life is all too real
When you have time on your hands
The hands of time move slowly for me
The clock never quickens or stops
A sound so quiet, so unmoving is the pulse of my time
Another day, another time, another place
A difference so beautiful
To believe this situation is alien to me
As I am a time-waster, a time-loser
A waste of time.

Leslie Bailey

The Doughnut Kid

His jammy face looked back at me
Doughnut in fist standing in a queue,
Eyes searching all the men,
He seemed to be searching for who?
Does he look for a dad? He had one when
He first opened his eyes and was new,
He had another but he didn't stay.
'Where do dads go? Shall I get another?'
His worried gaze turns to his mother
Nanas and grandpas come and go too
He remembers some, there were quite a few.
His sweet jammy face stays in my mind
One can but pray that fate will be kind.
To have one loving parent is one too few,
His jammy face seemed to say, 'I'd like two.'

S A Baker

Lonely Harp

Looking for an instrument of love to share duets
For long evenings of sensual sound
To hold my gentle form, move to life's rhythm
To weave magic through melodies

Write me love notes when we are apart
Tune my thoughts to yours
Our lives in harmony
Set my strings quavering

Sweet sounds to numb life's pain
Pluck me from this lonely existence
Strum my heartstrings
My sculptured body in your arms

Play my song, write new music
Share the warmth of reverberating dreams
Take this solo and build an orchestra
My harp in your hands.

Shirley Cawte

WHO KNOWS WHEN?

If sunrise or sunset you don't see
What message would you send?
Who's to say what will come this day?
Maybe an untimely end.
First on my list would always be,
Closest friend, my darling wife,
For helping me through so many things,
Like illness, hardship, life.
Thank you, I love you, is not enough,
So much to say, decisions tough.
Let's just say since our first kiss,
The time thereafter, total bliss!
Next to my children heed this warning,
I'd ask them don't forsake it,
Every day in life is precious
And is only what you make it.
Please try to set your aims high,
But keep targets within reach.,
Believe all times in yourself,
By practising what you preach.
To others all who know me,
Whether family, friends or foes.
If I had not met them,
Would I be writing this, who knows?

Jim Fraser

Tears For Beslan

I cried,
I cried red-hot tears, tears of anger and sorrow.

I cried,
As a mother, for those hearts now left hollow.

I cried,
For the feelings of loss and of grief.

I cried,
In frustration and stunned disbelief.

I cried,
For the children, young lives lost forever.

I cried,
For the parents at the end of their tether.

I cried,
For the pain of those who survived, and for the trauma
They'll carry for the rest of their lives.

I cried,
Selfish tears, I've no reason to mourn,
Compared to their grief and the terror they've borne.

I cried,
For the town in its now empty calm.
Life won't be the same for the folk of Beslan.

For whatever the reason, their foe thinks they've won,
But you can't win a war by killing the young.

These were innocent people who shouldn't have died,
And for that very reason, I cried and I cried.

Audrey Harman

DEAR SWEETHEART

(To Teg, you are my . . .)

I cherish our moments together,
like grass and flowers are married with dew,
I feel our hearts are entwined as one,
and happiness is through and through.

Our love is unique and only,
nothing can break that bond,
like flowers swaying gently in a summer breeze,
and water slowly rippling on a clear blue pond.

Although I may not have much to give,
my love, it is always there,
I'll wrap you up in my arms,
and warm you with my loving care.

I am your mate, I am your pal,
I'm also your true friend,
and all my heart and love for you,
from my soul I send.

Peter Bayliss

FAMINE

You turn on the television, what do you see?
Destruction and decay, looking back at me.
The street full of dust, with debris on the ground,
Malnutrition shown on the bodies, they have found.
Villages deserted, people walk for miles,
Just for food and water, plus medical supplies.

They have no food or clean water, to live from day to day,
We feel so sad and helpless, watching them fade away.
They look so gaunt, terribly thin,
Their bodies protruding, through their skin.
Their big brown eyes, pleading with you,
'Please help us, tell us what to do?'

Cries of hunger, all around,
Old and young, lie on the ground.
Bellies enlarged with malnutrition,
Bowls of rice, that's all they're given.
They have no energy to flick the flies,
They land on their bodies, and in their eyes.
It's such a sorrowful sight to see,
These lovely people, dying in front of me.

No medicine to ease their pain,
Their sad faces, etched with strain.
They always seem dignified and composed,
What a terrible way to go!
Stop the fighting, let them live!
A simple life is all they ask,
Clean water, food and work, please give.

Marilyn Pullan

A Colourful Story

I'll tell you what to do
Be imaginative and bright
There's no need to be true
There's no need to be right

Embellish a little
Tell a few lies
They're all very thick,
They'll be no surprise

Make it sordid and blue
Dangerous and brave
They'll all follow you
And your stories they'll crave

You'll be the king of kings
Amongst your fellows
They won't say a thing
They're all too yellow

But what if it all fell down?
If someone came and removed your crown?
If your waters became muddy and brown?
Then wouldn't you look a clown?

Cos, hold on a mo
I'm not that green
And by the way, I know
So say what you mean

Cos I've no time for your drivel
And I've no time for grey
So on this digit you can swivel
Cos I mean what I say

Why do you mingle?
What's wrong with what's right
When it's all very simple?
It's all black and white.

D Winkle

THE STORM

The mighty wave which came by night
While thunder raged and lightning striked
The rain lashed down, the wind was blowing
And everywhere, fires were glowing
The sky darkened all around
And the raging storm did shake the ground
The clouds scudded swiftly across the sky
So big, so bold, they seemed so high.
The storm has passed, stars bright and shiny
Sparkle like diamonds on the briny.

Graham Gordon

Our Baby

Bonny blue eyes and golden hair
Your rippling laughter everywhere
Gurgling and chattering you always seem
Filling the house with bright sunbeams.

As you toddle around the room,
Chatting in a crooning tune,
Down you tumble, up you get,
Now your eyes with tears are wet.

When your busy day is over,
Back to your cot you go once more,
In white apparel in slumber deep,
Safe in the loving arms of sleep.

Gertrude Curley

WHENEVER

Whenever you feel lonely
Whenever you feel blue
I, my sweet angel, Linda Marie
Will always be here for you
And should any tiny teardrop
Fall from your angel-blue eyes
I, my sweet angel, Linda Marie,
Will always be here to dry them all
For I, my sweet angel
Love you so much
And I could never let you go.

So should you, my sweet angel,
Ever feel sad or lonely,
Just give me a call anytime
And I'll be there by your side
To take both the sadness and loneliness
From your angel's heart and life
And bring, if I can
A wide and bright smile
To your beautiful angel's face
And fill if I can, your angel's heart
Once more with happiness.

Donald John Tye

WHAT IF?

'What if', two words that haunt us all,
What if I hadn't missed that call?
What if I haven't locked the door?
What if I'd learnt a little more?
What if I hadn't had that drink?
What if I'd had more time to think?
What if my train is running late?
What if it's past its sell-by date?
What if I'm lost along the way?
What if my life should end today?
So why what if, instead, why not
Enjoy this precious time we've got?

Mark L Moulds

My Favourite Foods

My favourite food is jam,
I love eating it with ham.
I quite like to eat toast,
Just after I have eaten my Sunday roast.

But my absolute best is a sandwich,
With grated cheese,
A smothering of peas,
And a dollop of ketchup.

I once tried a lovely sandwich,
With sugar, Smarties and salmon spread,
All held together with buttery bread.
And a dollop of ketchup.

I also like flan,
Home-made by Nan
She fries it up in her frying pan,
And adds a dollop of ketchup.

My second favourite is cheese and onion crisps,
With a splash of honey,
But I only like it runny,
And a dollop of ketchup.

But my all-time favourite is
Ketchup!

Joanna Barton (11)

Any Subject, Any Form

Any subject, any form, is the editor's request
Well, I sat about for hours and hours,
What was I going to write this time?
All I kept getting was a mental picture of flowers!

A meadow so sweet of waving red poppies
So bright against the golden corn,
The image shifts in kaleidoscopic action
And I'm picking bluebells on a misty morn.

Oh, I can smell their sweet perfume, sniff!
Come into the picture with me,
Springtime, a sea of waving blues and greens
How beautiful is this sight to see?

It's slipping again, pansies smiling nearby
In the hazy background, roses bloom,
As I focus now upon velvet petals here and there
How soon their perfume fills my room.

A myriad different hues are mine to see
From white to gold, from pink to violent red,
What a way to daydream, what next?
Such enticing things filling my head.

Any subject, any form, really must awake
Black print on white screen, cursor flashing,
It seems to be saying, *'Wake up!'*
Oh no! Computer *crashing!*

Sue Meredith

INVISIBLE

Just a small terraced house in an old city street
Part-drawn curtains reveal a man crouched in a seat
Grey-haired, grey-suited, stiff collar and tie
Oblivious of the glances from each passer-by.
Before him his meal - tasty cheese, crumbly bread
He is not at all interested - hands cupping his head.
His tear-dampened eyes see only a chair
Left vacant by his loved one - no longer there.
As he bites his bread he still hears her quip
'Your hankie! Wipe those crumbs off your lip.'
It's near visiting time - the thought brings a smile
In the hospital ward - he'll be there in a while.
Holding her hands and smoothing her brow
Remembering the day when they both took their vow.
His dry twig-like frame rises to tackle the task
Of carrying his 'treasures' - some cake and a flask.
And - now at her bedside - does she know he is there?
Memory robbed by dementia. He sighs in despair.
He adores her still though she seems as another.
Ever nursing the hope that one day she'll recover.
Parting kisses, gentle hugs - time now to depart
Invisible, unrecognised - weary at heart.
He wends his way home to pray and to yearn
Ever hoping that one day, she may return.

Eric E Webb

UNTITLED

C andles glowing with a bright flame,
H eavenly choirs singing,
R obins with red breast in the garden almost tame,
I ce frozen o'er ponds and icing on the cake,
S tockings overflowing with goodies,
T insel of many colours
M istletoe and holly
A ngels complete with haloes and wings,
S anta's grand entrance into the living room

R equired is freedom from hunger,
E nding of suffering and pain,
C hoosing of good rather than evil,
I nnocence of the Child Jesus,
P eace on Earth,
E nter the magic.

Pat Seddon

Hurt Is . . .

Hurt is not being able to walk,
and not being able to talk.
Hurt is to see a child cry,
but you're unable to ask why.
Hurt is when you can't get anywhere,
unless somebody pushes your chair.
Hurt is when people stand and stare,
because they think you're not all there.
Hurt is being unable to speak your mind
when people are very unkind.

Marie Watts

STILL LIFE

Early rose of summer, picked in its prime
Fresh fragrance of untainted warmth.
Stands upright, erect, in pottery of human creativity.
Early-picked apples, crisp to the mouth
Cold to the touch, unspoilt by late sun.
Fruit and flowers contoured by nature
Filling the senses with wonder
Each to its season.
As with Man, moving silently forwards
honed by circumstance, mores and external forces
Seamlessly onward, assimilating experiences.
From inception to fertilisation
From conception to flowering
Petals drooping, fruit withering
as the process of regeneration becomes reality.

Gael Nash

They That Were Young

They will rise with the morning sun
Their spirits float like clouds in the sky
They never will be forgotten
Our tears will be like early morning dew
Their memories will lift our hearts
They never will be forgotten
Every flower, every tree
Will be in memory of them
They that were young
Will stay young
We will never forget them.

John Edney

Building Blocks

When we were young in summer
    we built castles on the beach
                                        -   one each

When we were eager students
    we built castles in the air
                                        -   so fair

When we grew up and married
    we built homes with hope and love
                                        -   such love!

Now we are old, we build no more;
    we walk instead through memory's door
        and stroll through golden days galore
                                        -   once more . . .

Patricia Fallace

THINKING OF YOU

I still think of you and yearn for the fun and joy
That might have been
Our love it seemed would last forever and never
Could be mean

We hugged and kissed and billed and cooed whilst
Dreaming of our future
The way ahead would be firm and strong held tight
By a fine-edged suture

But you must have lied whilst whispering of a love you
Did not feel
Otherwise why could you go and from our life so
Coldly steal?

Now restlessly dreaming in my lonely bed
I think of the promises that once were said
And the love that was callously thrown away
Leaving me lonely every single day.

Royston E Herbert

Some Day

The rain falls without a sound
Dripping down my neck,
I pull the collar higher
But it has no effect,
Through the soles of my worn-out shoes,
The cold and wet creep in,
Tears fall like silent rain,
No one can see my heartbreak and pain,
These troubled times in which I live,
Wish could go and never come back.

'Thank you Madam,'
'Thank you Sir,'
As coins are placed in my hands,
Time to find a place to rest
Ready for the morning, when regarded
As just a pest.
How did I let it get to this
So far away from home?
Why, oh why, can't I go and just pick up the phone?
I know they'll understand,
I lie down and cover up with papers, boards and rags,
A misty fog invades my mind,
A sense of being unreal,
The phone box is now far away,
Some day it will be real.

Mary Neill

Sorrow And Despair

As I look upon your face
I see sorrow and despair.
Eyes full of pleading
but hope no longer there.
How do I find the words
as I feel your silent plea?
For you are a stranger
someone still unknown to me.
Sadly I remember
another place and time.
When sorrow and despair
two words, that once, were mine.
To share this poignant moment
how sad that it should be.
You share it with a stranger
the stranger, who is me.

Vi Fazackerley

Poor You

Starry cross astride a steeple
poverty's gospel paupers' people
rich in rags and righteous groan
all that's mortal makes it home.

Cardboard box and Arctic cold
Miss Fortune's coffin sick and old
once when young she ran away
the streets were paved with gold they say.

While others kiss 'neath mistletoe
her fairy lights have failed to glow.
Santa's sleigh bells fall asleep
in crumpled, crushed and hushed-up heap.

White hair like a Harpy's shawl
vultured veins, vampiric pall
stubbed-out toes and rancid dress
dignity's ignominious guest.

Wait awhile and even pray
watch her while she pass away
or charge your glassy eyes with beer
. . . and thank the Lord that you're still here.

Sean Kinsella

WILL TO LIVE

(Dedicated to my wife Mary, October 1998)

I don't know what I would do
If I were to lose you
The magic spell that led me
To meet you
And make you a 'must'
Would, like iron, corrode
And crumble to rust

From all the others
Fine and fair
I knew you'd be
The one to care
Advice from friends
I got, good and bad
If you'd turned me down
I would have been sad

It's been so long
Since we've been together
I've started to think
It will be forever

If you leave me now
My heart would shatter
Like a broken glass
And the tears and the pain
Would soon come to pass

So, darling, please don't die
And leave me alone
I would wither away
To skin and bone
And if love knocked again
There would be nobody home.

James Valentine Sullivan

Universal Light

Reflects on the universe
A wonderful sight
Without the sun, moon and stars
The Earth would have no light.
Moon reflects the light from the sun
Moon has always done this
Since the world began
Take a look around, what do you see?
Reflected light produces a glamorous
Garden scene, with beautiful trees.
Rivers, streams, ponds appear
So beautiful in endless summer days,
Spring, summer, autumn, winter
Each new season we enjoy a difference.

Pamela Hopes

Just One

'And so
My learned friend
What is the purpose then
        Of feeding
One lone child
For thousands die a death
As silos
Groan with grain
In cluttered lands?'

'Your Honour,
One humble storm-tossed sparrow
        Falls Earthwards
And dawn-washed children wonder why God
Would let a sparrow
Die.

Yet in this vale of tears
    One candle
    Flame bright
Will lighten up the darkness
Of this tortured
    Troubled world.

'In minute particulars
        Do good'
        Says Blake.
One flame   one bird
One sheep   one son
One staring, starving child
These are, my Lord,
Minute particulars.'

Mary Froggett

The Bridge

Falling back over
I landed on the track

Splat, crack!

'A broken alphabet'

Said I looking at the
Approaching train
My thoughts are
Still registering

That.

Dave St Clair

Sideways Glance

Like Don Fabrizio I see
of the years of my existence, how few
have been actually lived. And I know,
at the moment before my death I shall
be less than attentive as I stare
into space or at the screen or find
myself diverted by a not quite
identifiable noise from the street.
Thus we die as we have lived:
by the law, if there's any such thing, of
inadvertency - the target missed;
'We are pleased to offer you the post
we're sure that you can live without';
misplacements of the heart; the praise
for what you'd anyway have done;
those sins of which you're secretly proud.

Ian Harrow

I WANT TO CHANGE ME

Life is an art,
you can become a master of the talents
you were gifted with.
To become better at what
you're best at.
Give your best and no one can condemn you.
To change nothing,
but that which belongs to you.

It's not important to win
with a competitive ego,
but to win for you.
And if I hit back when they throw,
I, too, am guilty,
though judged by now.

I would like to see all the
colours of the universe exchange smiles,
each one there for the other.
To see my brothers
and sisters
playing like infants under one roof.

I would like to see this
dark aura lifted from around us.
But alas,
this world will never be,
until each heart begins to say,
'I want to change me.'

Benvenuta Di Bartolomeo

A SQUARE OF EYE SHADOW

There is a burning in my chest
It is from sausages and cigarettes
And an aching in my neck
From the bee that was born there.

There is a crumpled plastic bag to my right
It has trapped some hot air so it clicks like
It has a half-dead fly inside. And something

Keeps falling in the other room.
But in the other room there is nothing
On the floor. But something keeps falling
In the other room.

The hand on the clock is red and ticks, ticks
While the men at the banquet hall across the
Street - they laugh and groan
And here I think -

Is no oblivion

That - is in the toilet
And standing there I think
I wish, just once, I could hear a woman say -
I've got to take a p***

To my right I can see the maintenance shelves
And her make-up bag has fallen over -
Out of its open mouth has fallen what has fallen
And as I leave - a square of eye shadow.

Ariel Beller

Pink Lipstick Kisses

Heroin, smack, the white goddess
of warmth; moves slowly.
Leaving a network of arteries
slow to respond, numbed, defenceless.

Words, music left unfinished,
stacked in drawers of light walnut.
A baby doll, of red silk, finds sanctuary
in a size seven white stiletto pump.

I light up in a non-smoking room
thirty floors up, empty bar, talking to
a stranger from the yellow pages.

Falling into a deep sleep; I leave this world,
with pink lipstick kisses showering
down. A musking of innocence stained
upon my sheets.

I leave this world . . .
bye, bye

James Scott

Losing Days

(For Jen)

'What's the date today?'
My professor once asked.

'The 23rd,' I answered
Absolutely blissful to rescue a goddess

'Where the hell did the 22nd go?'
My professor queried.

I searched my mind quickly
Drew a blank and I smiled ignorantly.

She caught the humour and retorted
'I lost the 22nd in a haze of stats.'

I felt like saying, 'Get a life and give me one'
But it jammed in my throat. Scandalous!

Come to think of it
We're two of a kind really
Stats do it to her
Words for me.

Tope Omoniyi

Then Is Now

Lazing by the quiet banks
Where willow stood as sentinels
I did not care to call to mind
My improprieties
- Save those which taught me love -
The unspoken words in rushed and pointless rage,
The unkind thoughts which did not heal,
The helping hand whose cost was weighed.

When those divinely authorised
Sought to instil in me the core of their belief,
I spoke in haste to quell the anger of that God
Whose shaft of light I barely glimpsed.

Now, with a mind that cannot comprehend
The Holy Trinity, the Apostolic Church,
Absolution through a simple act,
I can defend by argument
With words my heart can feel
To those I should have shown my love.

I, too, in time unknown
May sojourn in those lands
Where more than faith has taken countless souls
To unexplored eternity.

Michael Davidson

Questions

What is that?
Why are you doing that?
How does that work?
Where do they come from?
Why does that do that?
Why is that there?
When will this happen?
How is she doing that?
Can I have this?

Are we . . . ?
Can I . . . ?
Do you . . . ?
Have you . . . ?
Will you . . . ?

Who'd have kids?

Colette Horsburgh

A SETTING

How will I react to your death?
It's supposed to be a loss for me, isn't it?
Will I grieve for you, lament, eulogise?
A glossed and glowing, (aren't they always?)
'He was a pillar of society, good family man,
Always bought his mother flowers' eulogy?
Maybe I have mourned you long enough already?
No marble inscribe to tell me so. No date even,
No cards, no flowers nor sympathy,
For your life that never was, anything but a loss to me.
Several losses. A eulogy written for each, of not what
Or who you were, but who I wanted you to be.
So maybe when a future sun is at my back,
Shadow pouring from my toes, pooling - seeking you,
Tracing your chiselled name.
Maybe this loss will be, unlike the others;
Kinder, easier, shorter.

Mark Thirlwell

MOTHERS WAITING OUTSIDE AN EXAMINATION ROOM

Anxiously seated
On the edge of their chairs
Awaiting their darlings' results.
Mothers.
Clasping their handbags
Sipping and drinking
Furtively glancing
And secretly thinking
My darling is cleverest of all.
She can sing. She can dance.
She can act. She can do it all.
She's just like me but I never got a chance
To show my talent.
Who is that ugly woman?
Surely her daughter is not here?
And that other one
With a face like a prune?
Her daughter sing a tune?
And the other one
Wearing a religious hat
It's too ridiculous to think that
Her daughter could be wearing
Up-to-date style.
And that other hateful woman
Prancing about
Boasting about her offspring's
Delightful voice
When all she can really do is *shout!*
But now Teacher appears.
Three loud cheers.
They've *all* passed,
But . . .
Who was the star? Who was the bore?
Who was the apple of Teacher's eye?

With brains as large as walnuts
And potato sacks of money
These sad and wrinkled mothers
Wonder why life has passed them by
As they sit and await their daughters' results.
Pondering what might have been . . .
If they had only had the chance to be the apple!

Philippa J Sterritt

EYES OF THE SOUL

I watch you cross
With your garden that spoke of religion.

This landscape that feeds on
Waters of tranquillity.

Commitment to all -
This love and address.

To a watching benediction
From your soul and eyes
Of untold mystery.

Roger Thornton

A Carousel

Searching for existence in the puzzle that is me
I try to find reality; a reason just to be
Do I wear a smile today; do I wear a frown?
Shall I scream and shout today or shall I be a clown?

Will I have some purpose to take me through the day?
In this meaningless existence, will I find my way?
I want to show my anger; I want to show my pain
Yet when I try to be myself, I'm knocked down once again.

The maze of life's confusion leaves me right out on a limb
A search for true identity has made my vision dim
This crazy world we love to hate has left me standing still
There must be meaning somewhere, this aching void to fill

I need to search for answers but where do I begin?
A creature of captivity securely bolted in
The people who are close to me may say my soul is well
Is there a key to turn this lock; release me from my cell?

So, it's either on a soapbox or turn the other cheek
Would that make me strong as steel; would it make me weak?
Truth and confrontation might get me through the fight
But ships on alien courses float aimlessly through night

There is one conflict left to choose - silence or speech?
Both contained within my grasp yet simply out of reach
Silence shall be golden when truth alone is told
I will discard my mask today; risk it and be bold.

Judy Studd

Ark Of The Covenant

With a light that blinds
all darkness
And binds us to our faith
with an offering of goat's blood -

Atonement day is here again

Between the touching
cherub wings
A cloudy pillar ebbs and flows
as the Seat of Mercy beckons us

To acacia wood and burnished gold

Upon our destiny
we wait
The judgement of our Lord
for every stone that we unturn

Are tablets of the law . . .

And still the light is
calling us
From the shadows of our sins
to the tabernacle of desire

Just beyond the reach of men

And the Ark stands
like a rainbow
Shrouded in a mist
we owe a covenant to ourselves

To pass on all we have to give

For no one can ease
the passing
By the candlelight it's hid
in the flicker of a heartbeat

None can see the light and live.

Steve Gunning

POLLEN

The chair in the garden was facing the sun,
She sat there intending to watch the fun,
But started to shiver in the breeze,
Drat it, now she was going to sneeze,
Forgotten the pollen count was high
To stay in the sun would be fatal.
Sneezing was making her cry.

P Wright

Wishing Stars

I cannot think
Of a starless night
They throw light
All around me,
Colouring my life with enchantment,
Feeding my mind
With endless love,
Bringing contentment
To all seasons,
Companions to the moon they shine,
Beckoning me
To make a wish
For each and every day,
I see them come,
I watch them go,
A love of life
That glows and grows,
My wishing star
Is there, I know . . .

Margarette Phillips

Fame

sooner or later they take
the plaque off the wall.
small people point and ask
'who the f*** was he?'

words fade in libraried rows
unborrowed now since . . . really,
so long ago!

pictures fade in attics
cast aside,
half-remembered echoes of
'who did you say?'

except for children
'he's got his grandpa's nose.'

composites linked by dna
and faded photographs reveal
a web of history
travelling through our cast
of just-remembered time.

John Cartmel-Crossley

THE PEN IS MIGHTIER

The pen is mightier -
The newspaper verifies it
Plants climbing to the ceiling
Cry out for water. While
The heater stays on high
Shrivelling fruit in the bowl.
Oppression is real in the
Darkness of the floor cover,
The heaviness of perfume,
The dull lamp glow and
Drawn blinds.
Only the picture tells of
Nature - if only the
Water could stream through
The glass to the plant.
The newspaper states -
Stay at home, keep warm.
The pen is mightier.

Kathryn Graham

You'd Better Book Early

The eternal things that go on
in places like Vienna, Prague,
Madrid, St Petersburg, New York
and, of course, always in Paris,
came to mind as I listened
to this attractive, charming
young legal coolness charting
my last will and testament,
mentioning death and burial
several times like holiday
destinations you'd better book
early to avoid disappointment
in what's left of forever,
and where (if this marvellously
immortal and youthful lawyer
said so) I could find Heaven on
Earth and, like her, never die.

Geoffrey Godbert

Obsession

She leaves a note
Reminding her to wake,
Then she rises, writes a note
Reminding her to go to sleep.

Writing notes is all she knows,
He's tired of reading them.
She needs a note to remind her
That he isn't there anymore.

She writes another note,
Saying she's leaving a note.
If she doesn't leave a note,
She might want him back.
When she reads the note,
She remembers he's in Heaven,

So she scrawls another note,
Telling her to stop writing notes.

Dave Teakel

WELCOME

Welcome to my heart of fear.
Welcome to my pain.
Love was once inside of me,
But darkness it became.
Welcome to my emptiness.
Welcome to my sorrow.
Endlessness was yesterday,
And endlessness tomorrow.
Welcome to my darkness.
Welcome to my hate.
Blackness is my comfort,
And darkness is my fate.
Welcome to my nightmare.
Welcome to my game.
The love I once felt inside
Became destroyed and slain.
Welcome to my world.
Welcome to my hell.
Happiness I once was living
But darkness is where I fell.

Joanne Colling

VEILED SHADOW

Many people judge me by what I cannot do.
But I see myself as a chameleon who changes
Into many colours.
Look past at what you see.
Then you'll see the real me.
My many gifts and talents that
Inspire me to do so many things,
Are really me and no one else.
So judge me not, and accept me
For whom I am.

Tracey Anson

SNOWDROP

The time warp clock challenges blindly the rapid eyes of a silent
infinity, as the brutal rape begins to brain-sanction the time-trail plain
of a sparkling destiny under scorpion snows of Atlantic fire lighters
scorched by the maze fire fighters of the entrapping snare,
swinging towards the wicked snore of the silent window-lit sky,
which never appears before the red dawn over a scarlet sight
on ceasers' chiselled palace plight, spilling neon lakes for last talk
peace realms on frying tips of golden spires.

Where the jealous fallout of our web pyre deceases the sire limb of
sparrow eye children, and dead wire fracture lines inside the urn of big
foot's chronic kaleidoscopes where he sinks in shallow snow with
obsidian hopes.
A crossfire of glee lap lands wandering amazingly inside the secret
cave of the fragile knave.
As the fretless drones lie with the insistent spy upon the feathery rain
where all choir pain rots the Sellotape web.
Inside her white glass hand as the black beads choke inside the
snake's rattle, as he releases the silhouette flies to our own early
venomless grave.
On a grassy pavement where the bruised shrubs lay under an ashen lace
where we again see her nylon silk face, as we sit and crossly cringe as
the Eskimo bomb drops on our lithe silver tongues slivering as we
sadly express a whole espionage pop to stop the callous flies' melee
sop, as we unknowingly stain the princess's eternal snowdrop.

John Hogan

REMEMBRANCE

As we stand with our heads bowed in silence at the Cenotaph
on a cold frosty November morning thinking about all the young
men and women that lost their lives in two world wars.
They did so that we could be free of tyranny, live our lives in peace;
they gave us so much but all we can give them is so little.

Robin Morgan

A Housewife's Lot

A blushing bride arrives at church in style,
Looks radiant as she walks down the aisle.
Though she strives to be bright and breezy,
A housewife's lot is far from easy.

Besides full-time work she has to cook,
There isn't time to sit and read a book.
Then her asthma makes her wheezy,
A housewife's lot is far from easy.

As time goes by she becomes pregnant,
And she longs to hold her new infant.
Morning sickness makes her queasy,
A housewife's lot is far from easy.

Baby keeps her busy day and night,
She worries she's not doing things right.
Alas, her smiles are often cheesy,
A housewife's lot is far from easy.

I'd love to put my feet up, she sighs,
Each and every day the time just flies.
She dreams of rafting down the Zambezi,
A housewife's lot is far from easy.

Rosemary Davies

My Right In Me

A calm a lead for me
I won't take life casually
I'll fight for the right in me
Honour me if you please
I'll make a stand
I'll take one's hand
Gallop my steed
Run at full speed
Fight for the right in me
I'll pledge my allegiance to the Queen
I won't sit back and be mean
I'll get and fight for the right in me to be free.

J Evans

I THOUGHT . . .

I thought if I'd be thinking of you on my knees I'd keep you inside me
the way patience balances stones along the Ialomitza river

I thought if I'd kept my hands in prayer I'd hold you
the way stillness of stones does not scatter but has weight.

I thought if I'd be silent you'd hear me
the way love does when made quiet by the lips.

I thought if I'd stayed behind you I'd be close
the way shadow has a place through its intensity.

I thought if I'd buried my love under stones - a Midas' secret -
                                                  it would become precious
the way the ripened field is the touch of summer turned into gold.

Years on I am still unable to free river rocks from my childhood,
to match the sadness to its stone and the stone to its field,
to take back shadows from the mouth of sand.
Years on I still lean on words spoken long ago,
I still settle my fate with lines.

Elena Tincu-Straton

THE COSMIC DANCE

Start with a bow
Follow with a curtsy
Proffer 'How do you do?'
'In good health, thank you.'
And so it begins.
Attentively two minds reach out
With the gentle caress
Of exploration,
Connect across space.

We whirl around the stars,
Waltz on Venus,
Tango on Mars,
Rising up, spinning around,
Music heard by two,
The strumming of angelic guitars.

Aware of each other's toes,
Mindful not to tread,
As thoughts, feelings, opinions,
Interconnect over the cosmos.
And so it continues.
Two comets trailing sparks
Through the velvet dark,
As two minds
Connect across space.

Lynne Gilbert

LEAVE-TAKING

Let it end as it began.

Conduct me now the way I came,
back through your lovely garden.
Let's say how the magnolia is in full bloom
and lush against your tended lawn;
tremulous as something new and white should be,
the dawn of an immodest blush
delicious as a secret.

One last time, make that gesture
- so dismissive yet immodest -
all this is mine.

All yours, the quiet halls and chilling floors,
the empty rooms.
All undisturbed as though they never heard
the slap of angry feet or slamming doors;
ignored the broken glass - and that white paint
defeated quite the red wine stains.
All now is healed, restored and nothing raw remains.

Unlikely as the march of Roman Legions
are the vicious phonographs of voices here;
let not their shrill peaks pierce
the tranquil dance of dust in light.
Tread softly now - no startled whorls;
serenely past the ghosts who crowd the stair;
the tall stories of their formless grief,
hauntless as air. You may possess them, too.

Let's cast our eyes politely to the nothingness
just past that magnificent magnolia,
the subtle trespass of its blush invisible from here,
as though quite unbegun.
In place, pristine,
complicit as the distant, tended lawn.

T Down

The Shuttered Room

Be not afraid for the beauty that will go,
Be not afraid when your eyes with time grow dim,
When the sheen of your hair is lost in grey;
Be not afraid.
Do not fear that when you grow old and your body weary
That my interest will fade,
For all that you have ever been is stored away
Deep in my heart until the last day.
Do not worry, therefore, when you cannot leave your chair,
When the day outside is sunny and the shrill birdsong is heard;
In those days the beauty of your voice and mind
Will still be there,
And you will find me waiting in the shuttered room.

Paul Gardner

SICK AND COSTLY WENCHES

Now, I say, let no man be caught in that practice
that here strokes the moment but omits the grovelling passages;
that budding activity which preys upon reason and to it dismiss;
that incites extravagant fancies in our minds' counties and villages
so we swoon and shuffle drunkenly though we be not faint,
sighing sickly in solitary melancholy over dull fantasies;
that having eyes to see devils only see saints
and ears to hark calamities only heed the apologies
while we spend and spend and coat these deceivers in prime furs.
Let no collector gather scarce creepers and not unlid the jar
nor busy vixen, after wages at the pen, shut the door to its lair,
for even glow-worms do light caverns but in the morn will skitter.
And when we in our spending are spent and our sights return
they shall flee with their plunder and alas, another knave here
is undone.

Azuka Oyem

Counting To A Thousand

(To Chrissie Bousfield)

It was always maintained by my mother
That there was a bridge across the river
Between the bank and the garden-island
And thus recounted a local legend
That told of a love-struck, lonesome lover -
An Ophelia haunting this hamlet -
Drowned beneath the bridge; with which the fecund
River - receiving one river spirit
Wreathed in weed garland - became dimly lit,
Coagulated, and gave up the ghost;
Whilst the bridge, like a sea-going dromond
Of old, seemingly sailed to another
Shore; and as on that day of overcast
Sunshine playing hide-and-seek - I was 'it'
And still counting to a thousand . . .

R J Stallon

Fairways

The cool crisp air bites through my breath
And the trees wave with their arms stretched out
Little marks can be seen from others before
A squirrel passes briskly with haste and some doubt.
As the clouds dance their way through the sky up above
And I climb up the hill to where the green sits
The ball stands proudly on the big great stage
Just another good shot in a series of hits.

So it's off once again and on the next tee
Long and narrow is the fairway ahead
A fizz and a buzz when it leaves at great speed
Bounces three times and then stops dead!
Not long now and we're on the eighteenth, phew
Tummies rumbling and legs a bit sore
Down to the last putt and it's in for a par
An enjoyable round and good solid score.

Jason Farrell

SILVER SHORES

Stood gazing at the unmade bed,
Peace and quiet on her grandmother's quilt.
Whilst comforting the sicky baby
She smelt schoolbooks and pens.
Dusty schoolbooks, empty dinner halls, lost friends
On her hands and knees cleaning the grate
She smelt the sea in the wind
The sour, sweet sea on the bitter wind.
She sweated over his ironed shirts,
They smelt of a stranger's cheap perfume.
For his tea she cooked egg and chips
They were ashes and dirt.
She drove to the shops in her child-friendly car
Death passed her by, on a journey on its motorbike.
She saw it wave, felt the sun in her eyes
And tasted tears on her tongue.
Fresh salty tears running on her tongue.
She was darkness and she was pain
But she walked on silver shores.
Just her, in white light on silver shores.

Shanni Jones

A Revolutionary Poet

I would have liked to see myself -
A revolutionary poet
A writer
A fighter
In the true sense
Whose artillery are words
Mounted on military movable battlefields
To charge and champion the cause
Of the silent and oppressed
Never to cease
Not for a moment, not for a flicker
Ignite to burn the soul searching self-revealing
Fire that lights
The dark crevices of the margin
I write
Through perils pondering
And wildernesses wondering
What would this life be
Had I been
A
Revolutionary
Poet . . . ?

High Priest

Crying On The Inside

(Dedicated to the people of the lovely little village of Boscastle, Cornwall after their flood disaster)

Now all gone those
loving memories and
treasured possessions
that were once our homes.
Waters, dark and rude
came uninvited, rushing
with a roar, our livelihoods
to carry away.

Yet now we will give
thanks to God there
were no lives lost, just
broken homes and cars.
We will rebuild after all
the mud and slime has been
brushed away.

We will smile and carry
on with things bright
and new in the knowledge
that old friends and new
will come again to see us.

So no one could see us
crying on the outside.

Julia Holden

DESTRUCTIVE TIMES

Nature at its powerful best
Not tamed by man
Polluted, yes
So they say
Powerful hurricanes, tornadoes
Ferocious in their destructive path
Destroying everything in their way
Mountainous seas flooding the Earth
Leaving debris in their wake
Floods all over the Earth
Sunny hamlets that are peaceful and serene
Then in moments are washed away
As though they had never been
As if nature is not fierce enough
Terrorists stalk the Earth
Killing and maiming the innocent
No one seems safe anymore
What future for our children
Surrounded by violence?
Families torn apart
Surely there is some other way
To settle our differences
To be able to live together in peace
As one gigantic family
Living together, helping each other
Let 2004 go down in history
As the year that we all learned
To live together in harmony
For ever and a day.

Patricia Turner

Prodigal

The elder son would have said to the Prodigal:
'Eyy Oik - Get thee to the cesspit!'

He had stayed with the father,
Endured it,
Resented it.
His stay, close to the father?

Far better had he argued with his dad.
Said: 'What am I doing here.
Doing this? I don't want to
Dragging myself through day after
Endless day.'
Dare he not find what the father really thinks?

Know what the Abba heart feels?

Irene Clare Garner

GOODBYE

You turned on your heel
away from me. I could not move.
You took six rapid steps
and stopped. Already
you seemed miles away.
Your back to me, you said
'Goodbye.' Then walked
off the soft ground. Now
I could hear your footsteps
on the shingle bank. Away,
away. My eyes stayed
fixed on the damp sand,
where six prints, like relics,
ancient offerings lay.
I could no longer hear
your footsteps, but I knew
you were already out of sight
behind the pine trees
and the white hotel.
And still the prints remained
until the drying grains
began to tumble in and fill
the impress of your heel,
the hollow day.

Mary Smythe

DROPPED

It skied, it flew,
Found light,
A shaded, drifting
Blur in blue,
Then dropped like stone,
Hit flesh,
Cracked bone -
And that was it,
Three runs,
The game was over,
Lost and won.
The Vicar prayed
Alone tonight
For safer hands
At cover.

Brian Parvin

TEMPLE RUIN

A wild cat stalks the pulpit,
Gracing winter's ice as
Thick as jackets. The
Remains of temple's grin,
Beams like a
Minister with trout's smile.

Tense muscles line the winter
Echo balancing stick insect
Icicles, the
Grasses stand rigidly in frost
As God replies as such to
Quality of prayer.

Only scarab beetle meets its
Piercing jaw, on penisula of
Religious rite
Like an open-handed prayer - a

Telescope positioned from the
Rubble of worship, like a
God pointing at our incautious
Stance with
Fury and with care.

Louise Wood

New Developments

Now they want to stop
local objections
to development plans.

Surely we must save
some local beauty spots.
It's power gaining control,
riding roughshod over
less powerful people.

Keith Murdoch

DREAM

Life is
A coffee
It's not
A dream

You put
The coffee
Into my
Cream

And as
It's stirred
All around

You're my
Dream
Upside down.

Tim Johnson

KISS

Your sweet lips on mine
A flaming scarlet desire
Ravaging my body
As it transcends to euphoric bliss
Your honeyed self
Penetrating deep into my soul
Your touch
Tantalising fronds of silver shimmer
Encapsulate my entirety
Whilst rivulets of starburst
Cascade through my veins
The ferocity
The intensity
Of this surging love
Captured in one tender kiss.

Mandy Plumb

Cotswold Tea Shop

One cannot help but overhear
Points of view from genteel table
Pleasant interest in a vicar
What has happened to whose daughter
How they abandoned Lower Slaughter
For Bourton, as tea, -on-the-Water

In and out of shops they saunter
Handling but not receiving goods
'Property is theft'. Let them be free
To look out through tinted glass
One stumbling block they'll never pass
The crime of being middle class.

David Speed

Tainted Romance

Somebody heard you'd taken my name in vain
Around this evil little town.
Come on my angel, was I really that bad?
You must have known from the start,
That we were sharing a tainted romance.

My beautiful angel, did you ever wonder,
Was I really ever human?
Or do you think I was the beast,
That was described in the Book of Revelations?
Cos I have to be honest, I don't ever know for certain myself.

But what I do know is, I wish I could take away the misery I caused,
Would you believe I cross myself each poxy night,
In the hope that all my sins will be forgiven?
We both know I'll probably be paying penance,
Every day for the rest of my life.

And as I stand in the cover of darkness, staring at you,
I wonder can you sense my presence?
God knows how much I love you,
And would give anything to get you back.
But I'm terrified cos I don't want to destroy what's left.

Cliff Heasley

See Yer Later

(For Jane)

In-built
Quilt,
But enough of such stuff,
(Interesting word that),
And Jane got the point
When I mentioned it,

Because she
(Apparently),
Was no twit
With the men,
(Much older she liked them),
Hmm, I missed out,
But still
You never know
What will turn up,
So see yer later, Jane,
Because right now you
Are on my brain.

John Binns, The Bearded Bard

Mr Rumble

He sounded like a lion.
He roared all over town.
He sang to the children.
He drank the pub.
He stole the cheese.
He didn't like maths.
    Will he like me?

Sarah Evans

Questions And Answers

'What did you do in the war, Dad?
Was it glory, exciting and new?'
'I was taught how to kill
Which gave me the skill,
To be here, to be talking to you.'

'But what was it like in the battle?
Were there bugles and drums busy playing?'
'When the guns start to thunder,
You just start to wonder,
Is it too late to start praying.'

'But what were you feeling when fighting?
Was that when the cowards were made?'
'A coward was a man,
Who was frightened and ran,
A brave man was frightened but stayed.'

'But when you were fighting and killing,
Do you think that it did any good?'
'No! What was the cost,
With countless men lost
And all for an acre of mud!'

'But if you were praying for victory,
And your enemy's doing the same,
If God listens to you
And the other man too,
To whom does He offer the game?'

'I wish I could give you an answer,
I don't think that anyone can,
He loves them, He loves you,
So what can He do?
Who is right in His Heavenly plan?'

‘But wasn’t it great to have comrades?
You speak of Joe, Charlie and Jack.’
‘It’s with sadness I’ve spoken,
There were hearts that were broken
They’re the ones that will never come back.’

‘Now I know what you did in the war, Dad,
And I know that you’d do it again,
Where bullies abound,
You will always be found
Protecting the weak from more pain.’

Brian Ellis

Retail

Entombed, crushed and stamped with human uniform,
Sleep weary attempts to claim more
Compulsion for possession, pathetic combat to have more
Faceless branding, meaningless reputation upheld.
Sheep-herding, pen to pen, bleating black sheep to grasp
treasured finds.
No rest for abused material food
No recession for the worn path of recycled shadows.
Independence exemplified by dependency.
Quality demanded.
No restraint until darkness claims a worn-out day.
Earned symbols bleed, the spillage used to absorb

Empty corners of a timeless space.

Karyn Jeffree

LIFE

The house where I was born, didn't have a lawn,
Or a garden to grow nice flowers,
We played on cobbled streets, washing lines were full of sheets,
And we had to shout our mothers if it showered.

Skipping games and shuttlecock, leap frog and whip and top,
We had to make our own enjoyment then.
Games of marbles lost and won but we did have lots of fun,
I wish that we could have those days again.

Once a week we had a bath, now it makes me laugh,
By the fire in any tin water container,
There was a rush to get in first and the winner did get cursed,
And they couldn't put their feelings any plainer.

I'm neither clever nor a fool, at fourteen I left school,
I thought my life would be in clover then,
Instead of days of milk and honey, I worked all week for little money,
And I knew I'd have to think and think again.

But Mam and Dad moved house again, to Silsden, here we came
To a bungalow with *a bath and hot water!*
There had never been such times, we could hear the church bells chime,
'Twas here I met the old Town Crier's daughter.

Doris is her name, I fell in love, I wasn't to blame,
I took her umbrella so I could have a date!
But she said, 'I'll tell my dad!' that made me feel so bad,
I gave it back but I knew I'd met *my mate!*

World War II, it's past, it's over, there's 'Bluebirds Over Dover'.
I go looking for my 'umbrella girl'.
I'm so glad it's *yes* she said and we both went off to wed.
Now after fifty years, my head's still in a whirl.

Charlie Peachey

WHAT AM I?

(For Reece and Michael)

Who do you see?
Am I a fern?
Am I a pine?
Am I an oak?
Who do you see?
    What kind of bloke?

Am I like water?
Am I like rain?
Or like ice, maybe?
A dried up stream?
    What do I seem?

Am I like the sun?
Or like the wind?
Does you mind think I'm
Like anything?
    What do you think I'm like . . . ?

Someone like you maybe?
Like the common grass,
Or . . . something more splendid,
Maybe a ball of lightning
Which strikes without warning?
    What am I?

I might be a cloud or a light breeze
Just after a storm.
Then again! I might be the norm!
Anyway, who am I?
    What do you think?

Whatever's the answer -
It kind of makes you think!

PS: I might even be you! Cheers lads.

Daniel Joseph Kennedy

FREEDOM

Silently the white walls stare like ghosts across the shiny floor,
No sound to break the bleak stillness of the silent night.
Asleep, separated from others by a tightly locked door
The prisoner sleeps, dreaming of what was, is, and might have been.

Theirs is not the freedom of open fields,
Blue skies, the song of birds.
Of seeing the sun rise in the still morning light,
Only the feeling of loss, of liberty, friends and family.

The clouds of the night darken,
Despair descends the cold dark cell.
The rain, remorselessly beats down like a thumping hammer,
Numbing the limbs, numbing the brain, not easing the pain.

Was I not like others as a child,
Cheerfully laughing, singing, dancing?
Was I different - no one yet to know?
Only realising now as I lie, silently alone,
This futility of a sad and lonely child.

Anon

ETERNAL

The darkened silhouettes
Of two people in the moonlight
Kissing on a starlit plain
Chemistry bonding them
Together
Their energy's lighting
Up
The darkened night
All the stars are falling
Angels calling
Heavens opening up
With love chimes
Stars falling, dancing
In the wind
Leaves falling
Reflections on the water
Embracing
Shadows rippling with the stream
A lover's waltz
A tango in the night
Lovers in the mist
Deep in passionate kisses
Exorbing the moonlight's charms
The swans still and floating
Looking at a gaze
In the misty haze
Under the moonlight's rays
Endless days
Her red dress - soft caress
Tenderness
Spinning round and round
Kisses and togetherness
In this garden's love nest

Together - forever
Eternally - no sorrow
For our tomorrow
We are all the colours of a rainbow
A place we shall always know
So much peace, so much love
Dance our way to
The heavens up above.

Dean Riches

SMACK AND CRACK

Smack and crack
Well what can I say!
Look where it got me -
Here, straight back!
My life is f****d, I need to change
As this just seems like one big chain.
I need to change to make amends
Here, it's got to end.
So what do I do?
I've got to be strong,
I need to see this through.
I feel depressed and sad,
All this gets me so mad,
But I'll prove one thing,
I'm gonna be drug free
Just you wait and see!
I need to do this for me and my family.

Jemma Carr

The Kitchen Sink And Existentialism

Washing his own bottom by sitting in the kitchen sink
Caught between Voltaire and Kant disappeared from his outlook
Chasing a swirl on paper, after the seagulls left the shore
crying for chances, a personality chooses to review a circle in time
do its work-in-itself
No one retired, or to mask it passing, the personality that is like a ship,
old and worn.

Another rank and file member of society, observing in a cafe
Chooses to see a bollard resting on a cabin, left by builders,
as if it was a gun dug up from a site of relics.
Old philosophical values tumble and work on and are quietly maritime
like a fish using a tank, surveys the boundaries of existence.

Above my head, as if taped to a wall, on a plate pink daffs chase
large blackcurrants, telling me that the poetic mean is not lost.

J Alsford

No Answers

There are no answers why life is here
From the big bang, it slowly evolved for what reason?
Dinosaurs ruled for millions of years
And we have been here, how long?
Are we on the edge of extinction already?

There are no answers why wars happen
Why one person thinks he can rule the world
Dictatorship, tyranny, evil power
Why do brainwashed followers, idolise a fanatic -
A lunatic escaped from the asylum?

There are no answers to storms and typhoons
Tidal waves, earthquakes, floods or drought
Nature has her own plan
We cannot control the forces within her grasp
She obeys no one.

There are no answers to child abuse
Perverted in thought and deed, actions totally unjustified
They are insane, the dregs of society,
Unclassified and worthless pieces of sh*t
And the children cried tears of innocence.

There are no answers to these terrorists
Who martyrs they might think they are
They are inhuman, no feeling of guilt or shame
Sacrificial scapegoats for the pretentious bullies.
Power-mad b*****ds.

There are no answers to those incurable diseases
The plagues of this century,
With all our resources at hand, how can it be
Man wants to spend money and time on lesser things
Priorities gone astray.

There are no answers to famine and crop failure
Why the rains did not fall on the dry land
Millions breathe in the dusty air, a slow death
No morsel of nourishment to sustain them
While the sun burns in the sky.

We have no answers
No matter how many times we ask, why?
We will never know.

George S Johnstone

A Terrace-Boy's Thoughts

Joined with others in their teens,
Packed together like sardines,
Voices raised in chant and song,
A united, happy throng.
Clapping over heads improved
Songs like 'We Shall Not Be Moved'.
Someone's voice would soon intone
The words 'You'll Never Walk Alone'.
Scarves would sway between our hands,
Sound would flow across the stands.
To the pitch the players came,
To limber up before the game.
Away team first (good-natured jeers),
Then the home team (rousing cheers).
The match would start, the noise abate,
And everyone would concentrate.
All being well, the thrills would mount,
Trying to make our chances count.
As a good one slipped away,
To and fro the crowd would sway.
At some stage our team would score;
A deafening *'Goal!'* the fans would roar.
Thousands simply overjoyed -
Pure elation, unalloyed,
And pandemonium broke out
As everybody jumped about.
Then when we had regained our feet
The repertoire we would repeat
Even louder than before -
Come on now, let's score some more.
The game has changed in many ways
Since those distant, happy days.
For the better? Don't think so.
Disheartened, I no longer go.

One factor in forsaking it:
You cannot stand, but have to sit.
The atmosphere is not the same
When sitting down to watch a game.
Since Hillsborough (a tragic day)
Much that I loved was swept away,
And I'm sad in what I lack.
I'd like to have the old days back.

Anthony Hofler

Grandma's House

Sometimes I like to remember the time when I was small,
of when we went to Grandma's house, passed the tree so tall,
that grew just within her garden, inside the little gate,
'Hello Lanky Larry' I'd hear a loud voice state;
and there would be my grandad, up to one of his pranks,
and I'd reply back, loud and clear, 'Hello there Long Shanks!'

My grandma would welcome us, a little hat upon her head,
and then she'd take me by the hand and lead me to the shed,
to see the little kittens tucked up so cute and small,
I really think that as a child this was the greatest thrill of all.
We'd then go through the old back door into the scullery,
it would be warm and cosy and we'd have hot cakes and tea.

Then she'd open the little door which led beneath the stairs,
'Trixie' and her pups would all be laying there,
and sometimes for a special treat a little one I'd keep,
safe inside my apron and I'd sing 'til it went to sleep.
'Come on,' my grandad used to say, 'come out in the garden with me
to dig potatoes, feed the hens and give the rabbits their tea.'

I can still recall the happiness I felt out there in the sun,
picking up little potatoes as he dug them up, one by one;
scattering corn for the chickens to eat and gathering up the eggs,
stroking the rabbits soft as silk, hearing the thump thump of their legs.
Then as darkness began to fall and safe inside once more
with the gaslight burning brightly, he would open the door
of the little cupboard by his chair and inside let me peep,
at all his many treasures which he always used to keep.

Or maybe I'd go upstairs with Grandma, the stairs went two
different ways
and sit on the chest by her window and hear her talk of the old days,
of when my mother was little like me and what they used to do.
I never grew tired of listening and always learned something new.

Sixty years have come and gone and I'll never be young again,
but my happy memories of Grandma's house always will remain.

Mimie

Nocturne For Suburbs And Moonlight 1960

The full moon spreads its glow across an upturned bowl of scintric sky,
The wind's small, gentle broom is sweeping fluffy clouds from where
they lie and hiding them beneath the carpet of the hills.
An unsolved crossword frame, a suburb's light and dark
gives to the night,
Where angled streets, dodge in and out of light
Like children in the rain.
The houses sleep, or stirring, blink their drowsy chintz-clad eyes
And silence, like a warm, soft blanket lies across the town.

The silence starts and vibrates as one late bus grinds slowly up a hill.
Seats empty, advertisements stare at one another, still.
As driver and conductor wish for journey's end.
As power-lines above it ribbon down to where they change
Their colour, as the moonglow dims, to cool and strange
and quick auroral neon glare.
A flashing panorama of blue and green and red that seems to kill
the night. Bright rainbows measured, entered on a bill
and paid each quarter, to the day.
Theatres here and there are quiet and sleeping, now
Storms stilled, grim death arrested and thugs and lovers bow
To day's convention and sleep in beds of celluloid.

The wide arcades are dimmed.
The shopping centre's in its nightly trance
Saucepans . . . and paint, lie frozen under glass.
Clothing, food, cosmetics at a glance.
Model dresses, shoes, lawnmowers, side by side.
Salted peanuts, lurid magazines, bathed in brilliant orange neon ray.
Food for the body and the mind.
A grocer's sales promotions for the day.
Peaches, toilet rolls and soap . . . bargains in amber.
Taxis slowly wend their way, flags calling for a fare
And call in vain, among those empty streets that do not care.
Yet . . . laughter rings . . . and noise . . .

Movement, down the street, where in its own deep pool of light
Day's worshippers linger. A coffee-bar stands yawning at the night.
Coffee . . .Hot dogs . . . fish and chips . . .
The attendant at the chrome controls of his espresso, blinking, tired . . .
Dispenses coffee, cool drinks, half sorry that the juke box was rewired -
He gazes at his youthful clientele.
Against the wall, a fair-haired youth in sombre black,
keeps night at bay by feeding coins into the tight-lipped jukebox mouth,
once more to play . . .
A record moves out, then drops, and then spins . . .
The needle's slim sapphire, a stone in a pond
Spreads rings of vibration, the wires respond
The speaker accepts . . . then the eardrums, the feet . . .
are caught in a quick, throbbing triple-time beat . . .
Their clothes introduce a bright pattern of light
that weaves and rotates in a modernist rite . . .
A brittle but rhythmical active delight
While faces are blank, set with eyes black as night
The pattern spins closer and faster . . . then click!
The dancers break apart and somehow come alive, coins drop
and records change, then back into that mindless world of music
without joy they range
Then . . . click . . . once more! More coffee . . . ?

The attendant yawns and checks his watch and longs in vain for bed
A policeman wanders in for coffee, sees the dancers . . . shakes
his head,
Shrugs his shoulders . . . and wanders on . . .
And out beyond the rainbow haze of neon glare
The full moon slowly climbs the sky's long stair
And peers inquisitively through suburban window-glass
It cares not who sleep . . . who dance . . . who wander hand in hand
It watches quite unmoved as lovers kiss . . . or cry . . . or
crowds disband
Its life is just to climb and glide
Among the stars unchanging, changeless as day ends
And builds a bridge to pass from day to day as starlight blends

With cool winds to softly cleanse the air.
Then midnight sets the town hall clock to ringing out the hour
A chime that wakens momentarily . . . and drunks, to glower . . .
And return to sleep . . . day's end.

Olive Rosa Thomson

TRISTESSE - DÉJÀ VU

The embittered and chastised soul once again mourns the loss
from a caring mind:
failure as the residue of empathy - the sacrificial lamb
on the altar of life.
The pain of the cost of giving scars the price of innocent sharing:
destructive and bearing a finality.
With passion the wound is always re-opened.

No euphemism can preclude the blemished emotion
that yearns for former banality,
and I can only feel confused and aggrieved that God
has prevented me from extolling the virtues of Christian love
and compassion - to heal an errant mind and bear the cross
of amelioration.

I reach once again for the healing balm of time, in the hope
that its cup will be drained of the dregs of betrayal.
My alter-ego tells me there is no hatred, no prejudice, no revenge,
but only for myself, knowing the consequence was generated
from my own soul.
I can only atone and remember.

Frank A Zwolinski

The Nightingale's Song

In the large garden, the nightingale sang sweetly
Happy and glad he was alive,
The bees swarmed about busy in their hive.
The garden was large, and held many trees,
The student sat at his window sighing in the breeze.
I must find a red rose for my love he said,
As he got up slowly from his bed.
She was going to the ball, and had promised him a dance
For a red, red rose, and he wanted that chance.
He looked and he sighed, it was early yet,
But a red rose he must have,
A red, red rose he must get.
The nightingale stopped singing,
He felt very sad,
How could he help with this wish he had.
He flew round the trees,
No I'm white one said,
I'm yellow said another as he flew overhead.
He went back to the youth whose tears he saw shed,
And heard him say, 'Oh I wish I were dead.'
The nightingale shivered, and went back to the tree,
I can't find a red rose he sang sadly.
The tree said go to my brother,
There's one way he said, his red rose will blossom
But only when you are dead.
You sing in the tree with your brest on a thorn,
Each time you press your flesh is torn.
Yet you I must warn,
Not until your heart is pierced,
Will the rose turn bright red
And your life will be gone, and you will lay dead.
The nightingale went away, he really loved life,
But he thought of the youth with a beautiful wife.

So he went to the tree, sung his last swan-like song,
Then he sank to the ground
And he was gone.
The youth looked through his window
And what could that be?
For a beautiful blooming red rose he could see.
He rushed out and plucked it,
His happy heart knew what she would say,
She opened the door, so lofty she spoke.
What's that in your hand, is it a joke?
It's the rose you asked for
Such a beautiful red.
You promised a dance,
That's what you said,
Her laughter rang out with a tinkling sound,
But her heart was cruel
As he presently found.
Away with your rose,
I want to be rich,
Not live in a cottage
And my clothes have to stitch.
He left with anger
And thought of his grief,
I must be a fool beyond belief.
He threw the rose into the road
Where it lay dying, as people over it strode.
He passed the tree where the nightingale lay,
Never to sing his song all the day.

Betty Puddefoot

Image Of You

Enveloped by trees as I walk
Teardrops of rain cascade through the leaves
On a journey to the sweet earth below
The union, a hazy mist of delirious joy
Visions of you interspersed within the dappled light
Your image so real
Devouring me completely and rendering me breathless
Enraptured by the smell of your naked soul self
Body aching with an eternal hunger for your flesh on mine
Breasts as warm as sunlight
Lips so sweet and yielding
Your intoxicating aroma engulfing my senses
Wherever I am your image sustains me

Mandy Plumb

A Will Taken Over

He stares that long stare, piercing, preying and the dark plot unfolding
The lights are on inside but he's not home, he's somewhere else
His strained rough hands clasped tightly on the bar, a fierce
nervous clench
A dented mind, vacant of emotion or guilt, just a cold void
Save your breath, his mind is made up with no looking back
He serves the devil, the devil that swirls inside him and won't leave
No choices here, just commands and he has to obey
After all, money is needed for this journey and it's one way.

She awakes, the same time every morning, her routine,
A soft and shrivelled look, sadness, peace and laughter are there
With a tired gaze that travels back in time through the window
Her past relived, memory lane's heard her steps o'er and o'er
Tea and toast again, it fills the gap and wakes her spirit
Why should she be the one, the one that kisses the floor?
Her deservedness shows no justice, on her plate
A tragedy in store not a statistic, it's just a real shame.

When she felt that blow she couldn't see her look, he did
Her fear reflected through those innocent eyes, unknown to us
She'll survive and her memory will stamp infinity on her walls
No friendly black suits to be seen even on the outside, anywhere.
As life trickles through the contours of her cushioned canvas
Through frightened eyes a shadowed figure's seen wandering by
Paralysed with fear, the thousand yards glazed look is now here
No end to the journey of a will taken over, tomorrow's just another day.

Jason Farrell

Wisdom Maxims

Divine favour rests
on those whose
concerns are to do
the will of God.

A tender-hearted saint
will manifest the love
of God and exude
the fragrant aroma of Christ.

The extent to which
a disciple seeks the Lord,
reveals how much
he values God.

A disciple who
carries God's presence,
will effect
remarkable changes.

A true worshipper
is a true servant
and a true son.

Azariah Ephratah

Famine

Make the soils around barren.
Refusing something to yield.
The water has gone dry,
For morning dews no longer appear.
The inhabitants are dying,
For their places have been ravaged and desolated.
Strife and hunger have taken over the neighbourhood
A life is drastically drifting from that place.
Migration takes turn.

Okoh Moses Echeija

CHESS WITH GAUGUIN

There is something rotten
in the state of Poems.
Van Gogh,
'tis new to thee,
a self-portrait
hanging from no one's wall
that bears
the camouflaged thrill
like a crush of frost
painted on the morning.
Home to home,
the Energetic Trash
sell the flags
of our new standard language
where we join hands
in a circle
and discuss democracy
and her tattooed fist,
on four fingers,
selling *expertise.*

David Russell

A Liar

You know where you are with a thief,
You know where you are with a rapist.
You know where you are with a murderer,
But you never know where you are with a liar.

A liar is always someonc to fear,
A liar is capable of doing everything
To turn one's life upside down,
'So', turn not your back on a liar.

There is always a smirk on a lying face,
Evil is the word to describe a lying tongue
And I also think it is an abomination to the Lord.

A liar is someone who wears people down,
They even have two faces
And you'll never know if you're down or up.

All tyrants seem to be perfect liars
Who manipulate people at their peril
Then laugh at their success.

D Mullings-Powell

Smashers

They urinated on his teeth
in the mug beside his bed,
ripped his home asunder
for what he should have

saved for a rainy day or night.
In his pillow
they found her necklace, bracelet, watch,
even the little ring of copper
snare wire sealed in wax, he had

made to bond his vows of love,
when he chose Romance instead of Fortune
fifty-five years earlier.

They forced his teeth into his mouth,
candle-scorched his chest and lower down
as they roared expletive-laced
questions on the whereabouts
of the money he had spent

on bringing peace to her last
illness and a fitting funeral
with what was left.

They prodded him with splintered glass
from the wedding photo
and sacred heart picture,
but only found his dignity.

He spat out his teeth,
found the ring of copper wire,
and climbed back into bed
where her smile invited him
into a new meadow.

Tommy Frank O'Connor

WISHES

Persist with your wishes
Once again cut in two
Divided, our minds roam free
Nights draw longer, brighter stars and clearer skies intrude
The summer days bring chances alive for you
Mist and rain passed
Welcome, the smell of a fresh morning dew

Capture a picture
A shelter with no walls
Expose your temptations and fears
Before the wind of inevitability forces you backwards
And suffocates your will

Strengthen the mortar, lay the bricks of regret
You can change, today and tomorrow, conclude
Attract, seek, relax and embrace

B Manhire